CE LION. BACK AWAY SLOWLY.

BE LARGE. SHOUT.

P9-DNE-600

REMOVE FULL TRAYS

On Edge, Lift Using Both Hands

小心地滑

100

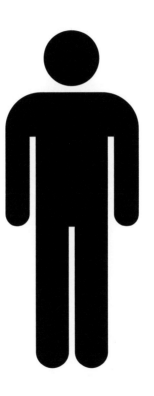

stick man's

steve mockus

illustration by funnel inc.

really bad day

CHRONICLE BOOKS

SAN FRANCISCO

For mom and dad, Sandy and Ali, Alex and Jake, and for Jody.

Library of Congress Cataloging-in-Publication Data

Mockus, Steve.
  Stick Man's very bad day / by Steve Mockus ; illustrations by Funnel, Inc.
     p. cm.
  ISBN 978-1-4521-1154-4
  1. American wit and humor. I. Funnel, Inc. II. Title.

  PN6165.M64 2012
  818'.602—dc23

                         2012006791

Manufactured in China.

Illustrations by Funnel Inc.
Design by Neil Egan

Endsheet photos by Steve Mockus except: crocodile (Tanya Knight), driveshaft (Eric Schoonover), falling weight (Tera Killip), mountain lion (Seth Golub), and whale (Cyndy Sims Parr).

10 9 8 7 6 5 4 3 2 1

Chronicle Books LLC
680 Second Street
San Francisco, California 94107
www.chroniclebooks.com

introduction

Stick Man is the guy you see around town, but don't really know very well.

He's seems nice. He gives up his seat at the front of the bus for those in greater need. He throws his litter away in the proper trash receptacle. He even indicates when it's safe to cross the street.

He also helpfully demonstrates, by way of warning and at great personal peril, what happens if you don't mind the subway gap, stray too close to the cliff's edge, slip on a wet floor, and improperly operate a forklift.

He has terrible luck. If something can go wrong, it probably will for him. But he also seems to have amazing recuperative powers, and he never gives up, no matter what mishap may befall him next.

This book illustrates a day in the life of Stick Man using images derived from real signs from around the world.

Everyone has days when nothing goes right, and every-thing just seems to get worse. But Stick Man's adventures show both what a really bad day looks like, and that in the end it's never quite as bad as it may seem.

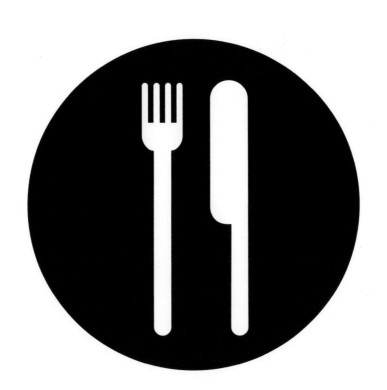

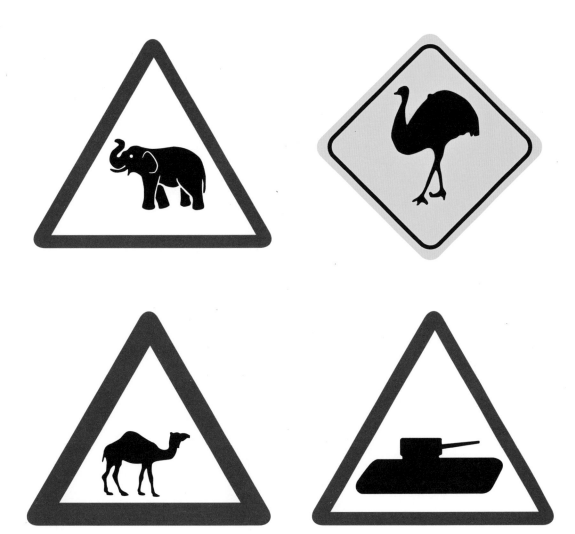

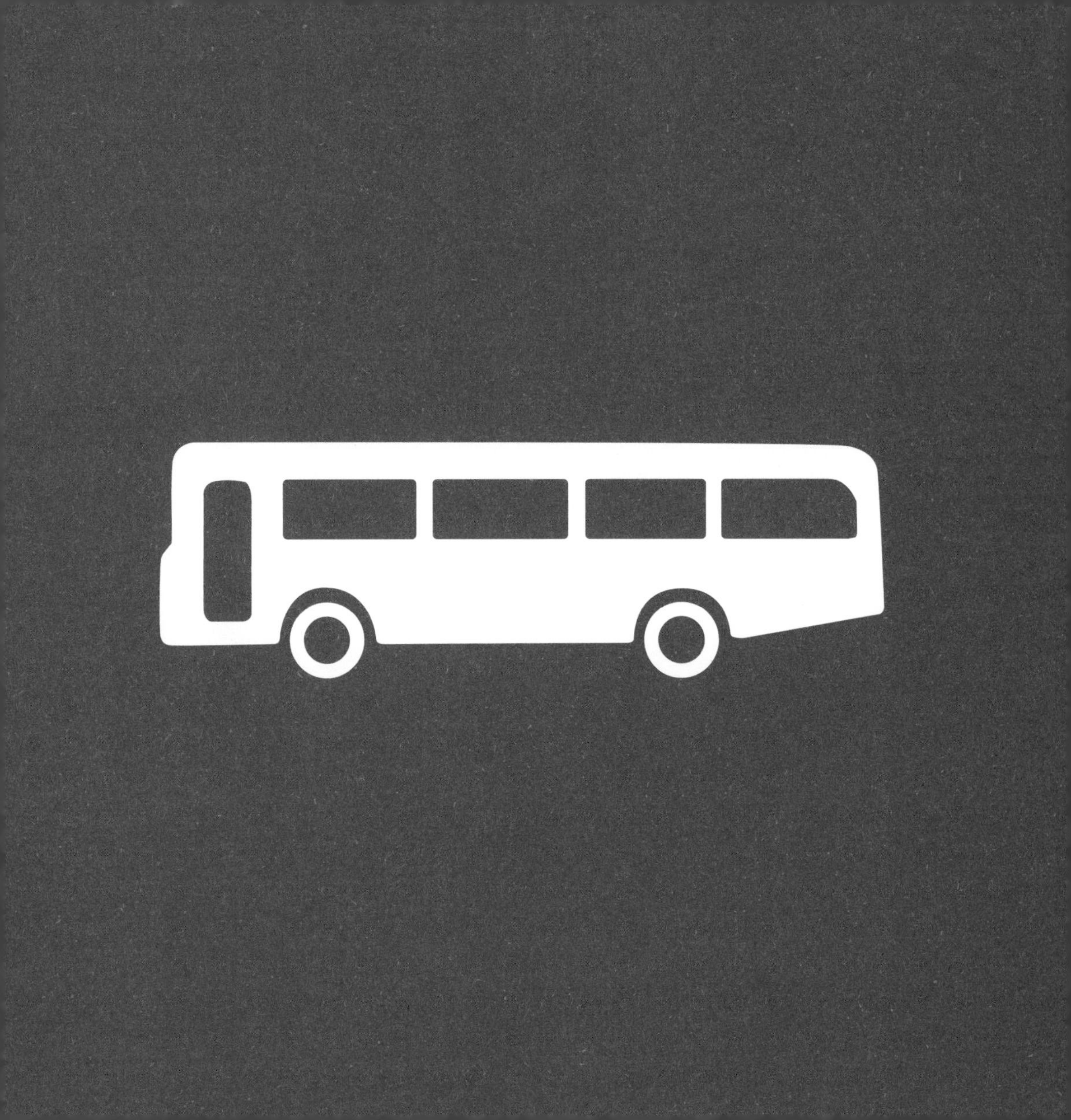

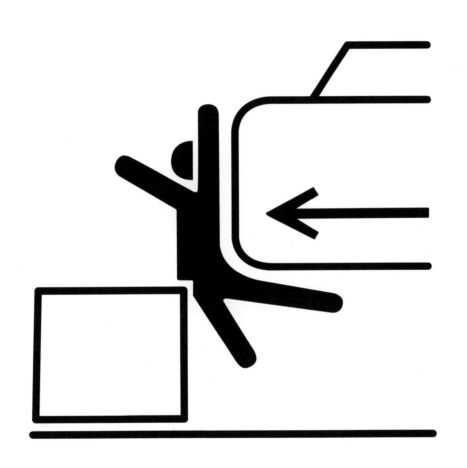

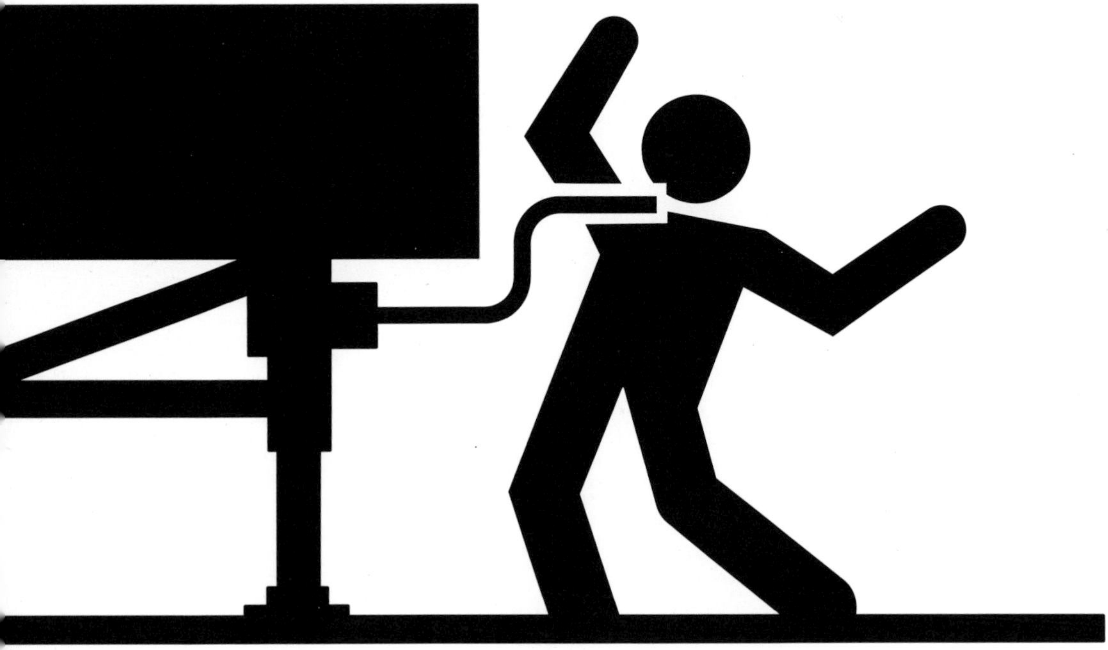

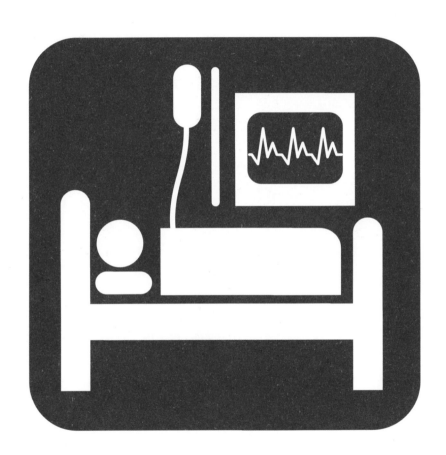

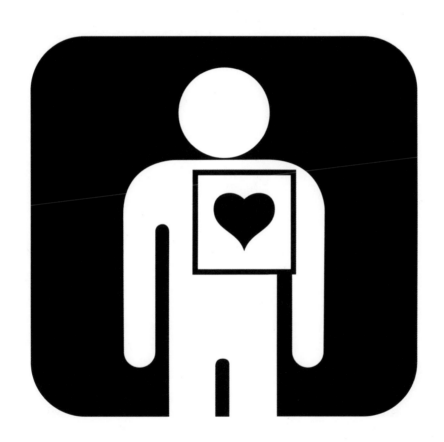

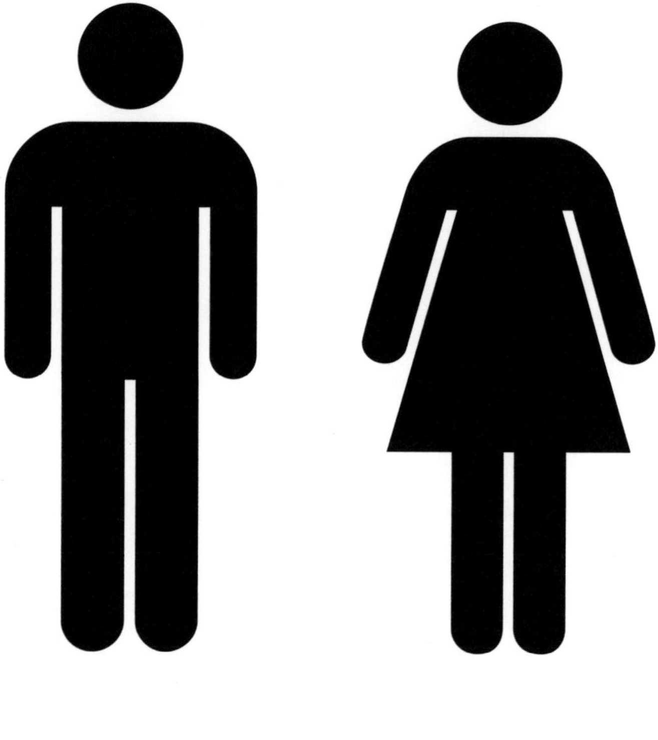

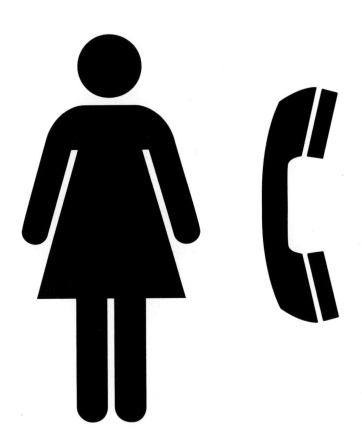

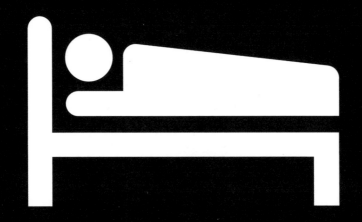